The Amazing Calendar Quilt
A Journey Through The Islamic Months

written and illustrated by
Zubia Imami Sheikh

Ta-Ha Publishers Ltd.

1, Wynne Road,
London, SW9 0BB
sales@taha.co.uk
www.taha.co.uk

This book is dedicated to my little ones Yousef and Nadia.

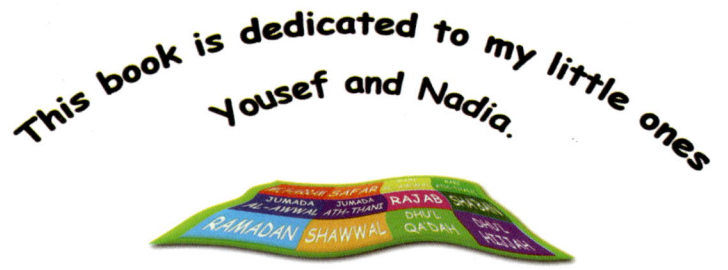

Copyright © Zubia Imami Sheikh.   1425 AH / July 2004 CE

Published by:
Ta-Ha Publishers Ltd.
1 Wynne Road
London SW9 0BB

Website: http://www.taha.co.uk
Email: sales@taha.co.uk

All rights reserved. No part of this publication may be reproduced, stored in any retrieval system or transmitted in any form or by means, electronic, mechanical, photocopying, recording or otherwise without the prior permission of the publishers.

Written and Illustrated by: Zubia Imami Sheikh
Edited by: Dr. Abia Afsar-Siddiqui

A catalogue record of this book is available from the British Library.

ISBN 1 842000 61 6

Printed in England by De-Luxe Printers Ltd.
245a, Acton Lane, London NW10 7NR

INTRODUCTION

Many of us are familiar with the Christian calendar, which is also known as the Gregorian calendar. It starts from January and ends in December. It has 365 days in a year with each month being either 30 or 31 days long, apart from February, which can have 28 or 29 days. This calendar is based on the movements of the sun (solar based).

Muslims have their own calendar which is called the Islamic calendar. It is dated from when the Prophet Muhammad (SAAS) migrated from Makkah to Madinah. This journey was known as the <u>Hijrah</u>, so that is why the Islamic calendar is also called the Hijri calendar. The Islamic calendar is based on the movements of the <u>moon</u> (lunar based). It has 355 days and each month can have either 29 or 30 days. Just like the Gregorian calendar, the Islamic calendar also has 12 months.

One Lunar Cycle = One Islamic Month

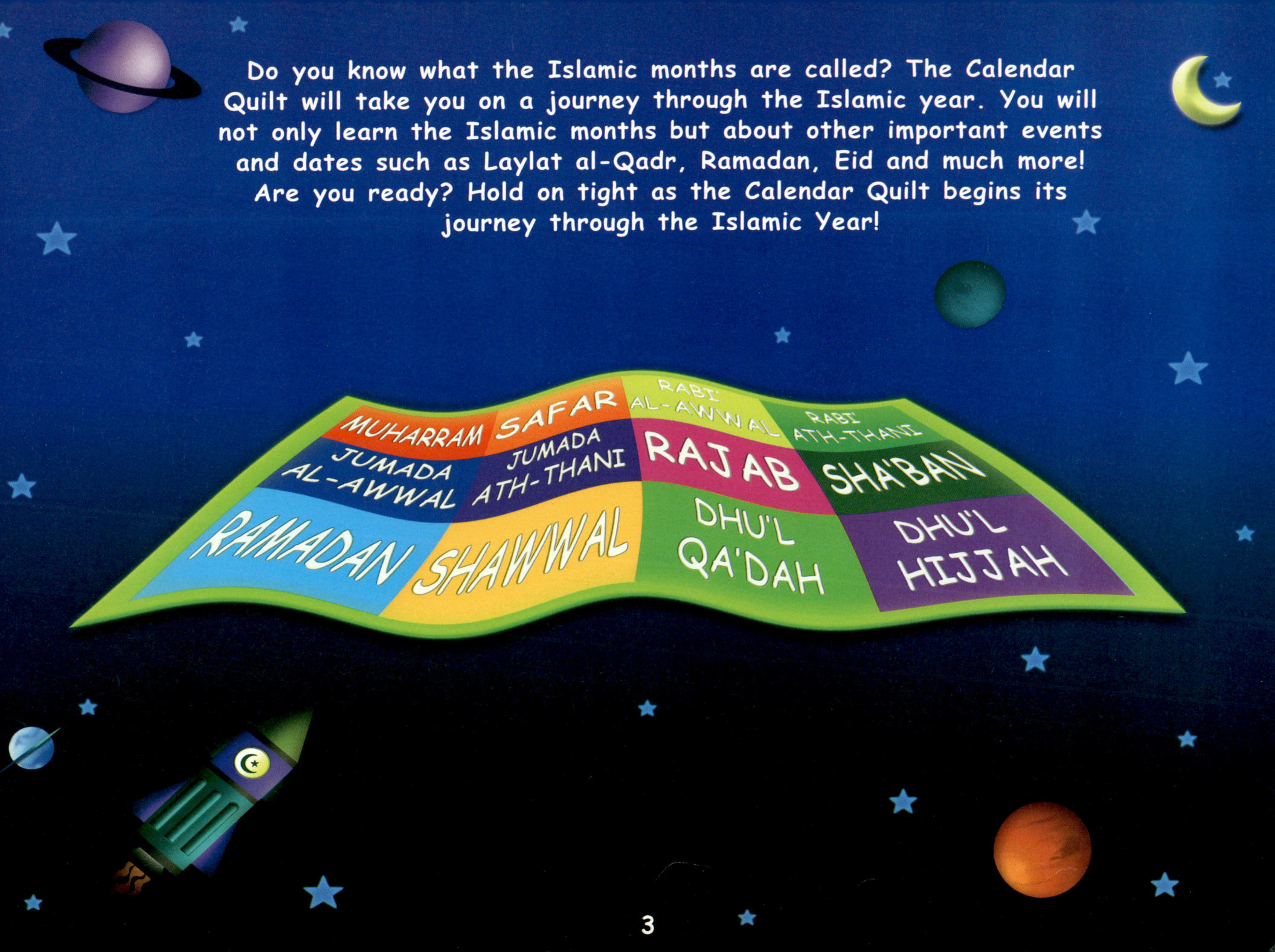

Do you know what the Islamic months are called? The Calendar Quilt will take you on a journey through the Islamic year. You will not only learn the Islamic months but about other important events and dates such as Laylat al-Qadr, Ramadan, Eid and much more! Are you ready? Hold on tight as the Calendar Quilt begins its journey through the Islamic Year!

MUHARRAM is the first month of the Islamic year. It is a sacred month. 1st Muharram is the first day of the new Islamic Year. 10th Muharram is unique because many things are said to have happened on this day. It is also called Ashura.

This was the day when Nuh's (AS) ark arrived safely onto dry land after the Great Flood. Many years later, Musa (AS) and his people, the Bani Isra'il, were saved on this very day while crossing the Red Sea. Pharoah, who was following them, however, drowned. This was also the day when the grandson of the Prophet Muhammad (SAAS), Hussain (RA), was martyred, or killed for his beliefs, in Karbala, Iraq. Muslims usually fast voluntarily on 9th and 10th Muharram.

SAFAR is the second month of the Islamic year.
This is a quiet month.

RABI' ATH-THANI is the fourth month of the Islamic year.
JUMADA AL-AWWAL is the fifth month of the Islamic year.
JUMADA ATH-THANI is the sixth month of the Islamic year.

"2nd spring"

"1st freezing"

"2nd freezing"

RAJAB is the seventh month of the Islamic year. This is a sacred month. The 27th of Rajab is known as Laylat al-Isra wal Mi'raj. This was when the Prophet Muhammad (SAAS) went on an incredible night journey that took him from al-Masjid al-Haram in Makkah to al-Masjid al-Aqsa in Jerusalem and from there up through the seven heavens to meet directly with Allah (SWT).

al-Masjid al-Aqsa

The journey from Makkah to Jerusalem is called Isra, which means 'travel by night'. The Prophet (SAAS) made this journey on a winged creature named <u>Buraq</u> accompanied by the Angel Jibra'il (AS).

The journey from Jerusalem up through the heavens is called the Mi'raj, which means 'ascent' or 'climbing up'. The Prophet Muhammad (SAAS) met many other Prophets, including Musa (AS), Ibrahim (AS), Adam (AS), and Isa (AS), as he journeyed through the heavens. Finally, the Prophet Muhammad (SAAS) received the command directly from Allah (SWT) for 5 times daily Salah on this journey.

SALAH
5 times daily !

SHA'BAN is the eighth month of the Islamic year. The night of the 15th of Sha'ban is called Laylat al-Bara'at or the Night of Repentance. It is said that on this night Allah's decision about who is to be born and who will die in the forthcoming year descends. It is also said that on this night we should pray to Allah (SWT) to shower us with His Blessings.

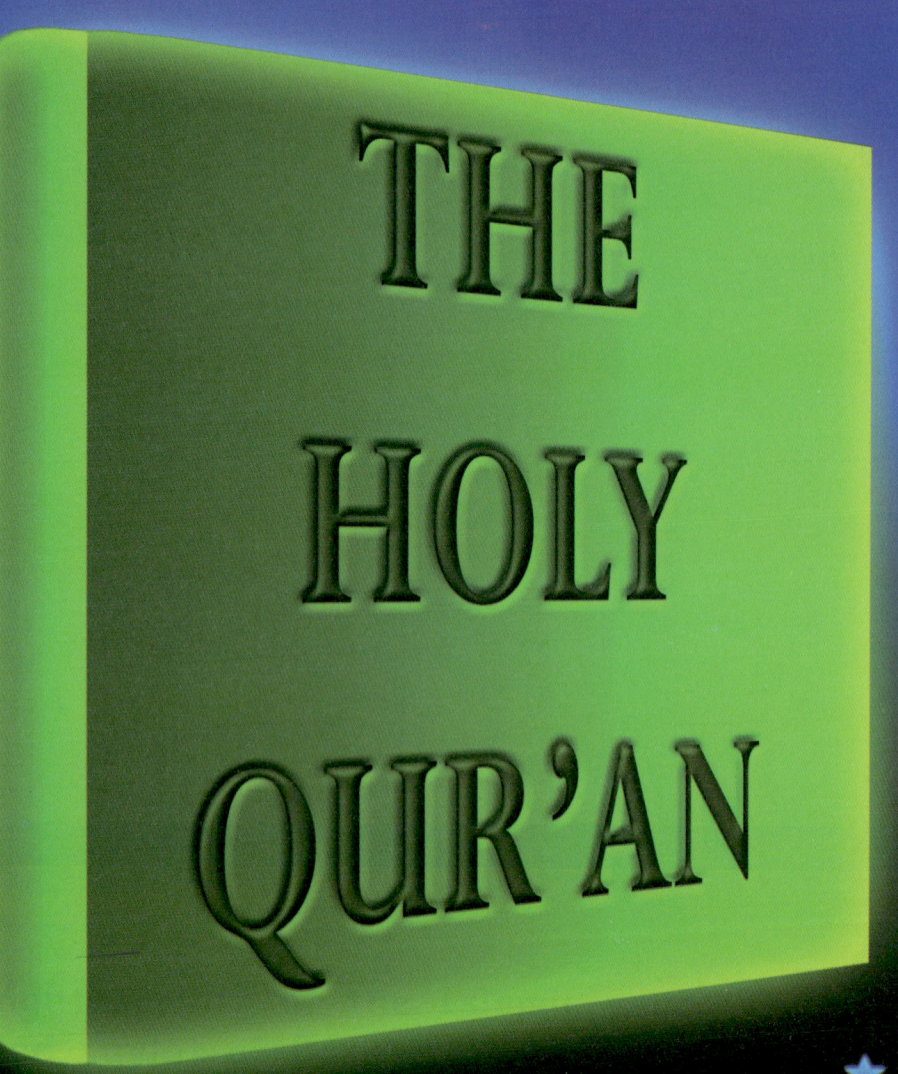

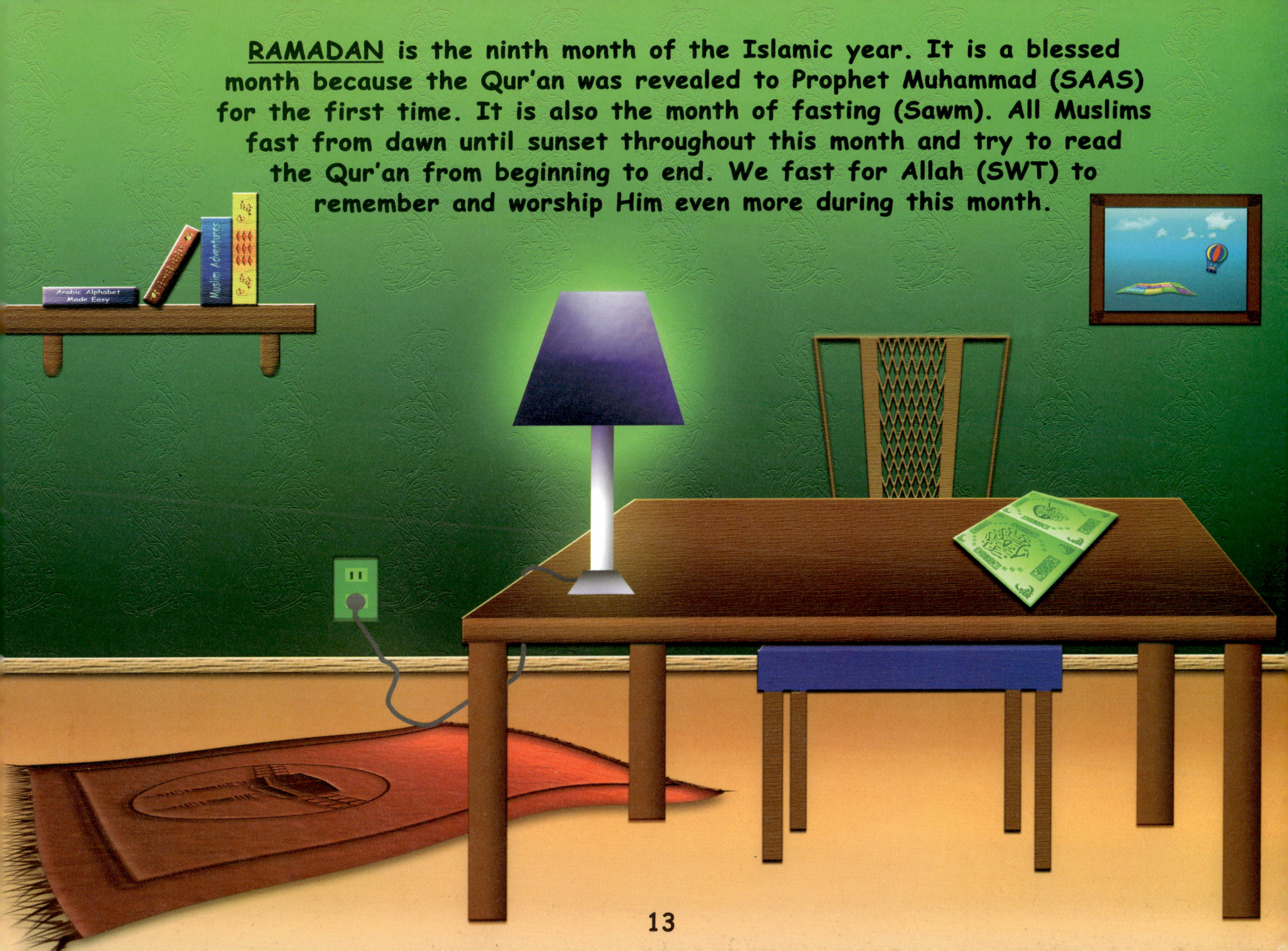

RAMADAN is the ninth month of the Islamic year. It is a blessed month because the Qur'an was revealed to Prophet Muhammad (SAAS) for the first time. It is also the month of fasting (Sawm). All Muslims fast from dawn until sunset throughout this month and try to read the Qur'an from beginning to end. We fast for Allah (SWT) to remember and worship Him even more during this month.

Fasting teaches us self-control and patience. It also makes us realise how the poor and hungry suffer every day, so that we can help them and appreciate what Allah (SWT) has given us even more. Every night, Muslims offer a special voluntary prayer after Isha called Tarawih.

Laylat al-Qadr, the Night of Power, is on one of the odd numbered nights in the last 10 nights of Ramadan. On this night, in a cave known as Cave Hira. The first words of the Qur'an were revealed to Prophet Muhammad (SAAS) by the Angel Jibra'il (AS). Muslims should pray to Allah (SWT) for his blessings on this special night. It is said to be better than 1000 months in terms of its rewards from Allah (SWT).

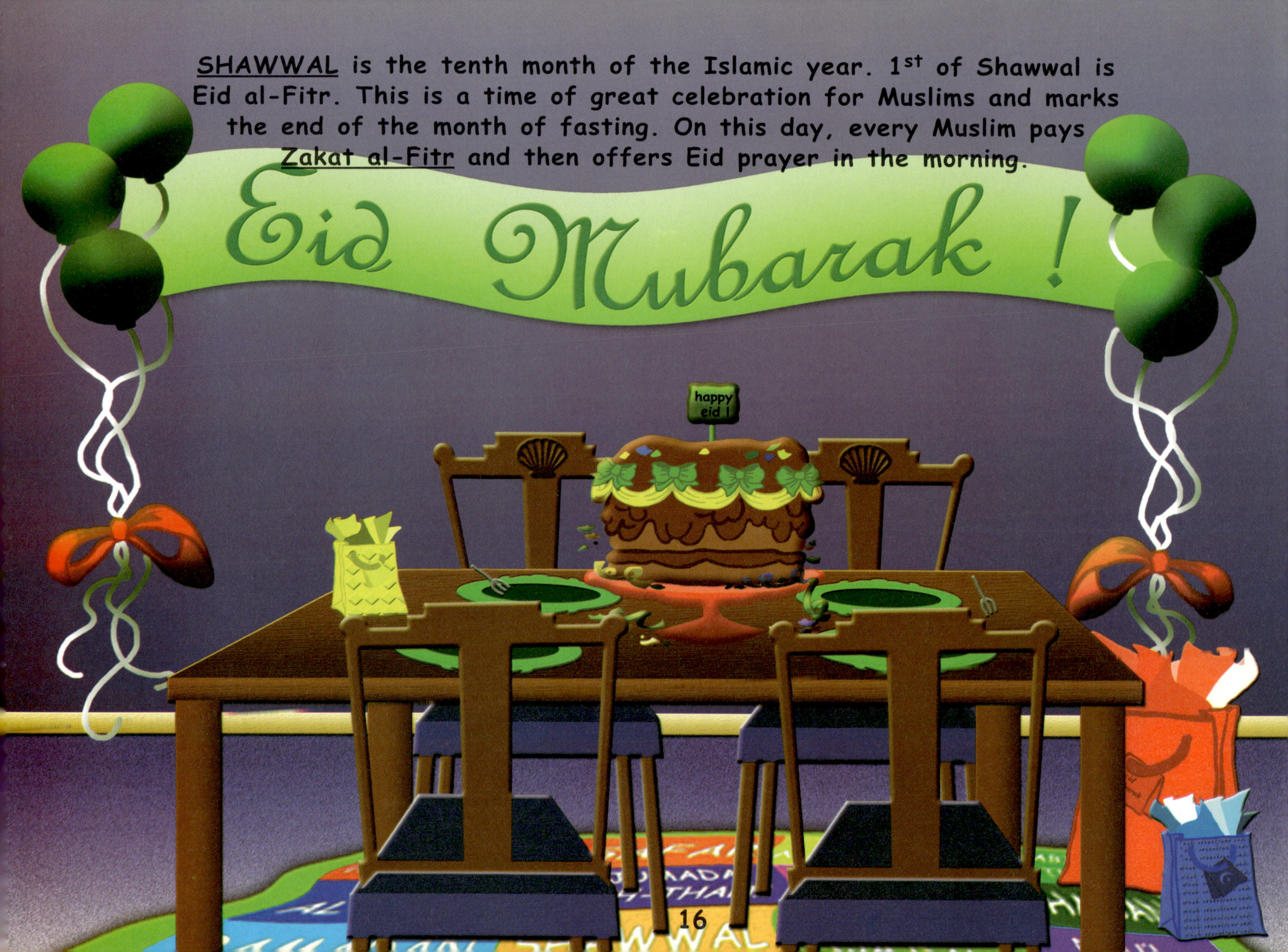

DHU'L HIJJAH is the twelfth and last month of the Islamic year. It is a sacred month and also the month of Hajj. Millions of Muslims from all over the world go to Saudi Arabia to perform the Hajj at least once in their lives. They visit al-Masjid an-Nabawi in Madinah, al-Masjid al-Haram in Makkah, Muzdalifah and Mina. 9th Dhu'l Hijjah is known as Yawm al-Arafah, and this is when all the Hajis gather at Arafat to ask forgiveness from Allah (SWT). Hajj reaches a climax with the sacrifice of an animal on 10th Dhu'l Hijjah. This is done in tradition with Ibrahim (AS) who was asked by Allah (SWT) to sacrifice his son Isma'il (AS). When he was about to do so, Allah replaced Isma'il (AS) with a sheep.

Muslims who are not performing Hajj can offer a voluntary fast on Yawm al-Arafah to seek forgiveness for their wrong actions. The following day, 10th Dhu'l Hijjah, is when Muslims celebrate Eid al-Adha. Eid prayers are offered in the morning. Then when Muslims sacrifice an animal, they share the meat with the poor, with their relatives and friends, and keep some for themselves. The celebration of Eid al-Adha lasts for three days.

Did you enjoy your journey through the Islamic year on the Calendar Quilt? Let's see how much you can remember:

1. How many days are there in the Islamic year?

2. Can you remember which months are sacred months?

3. Name at least two events that happened on 10th Muharram.

4. In which month was the Prophet Muhammad (SAAS) born?

5. What was the name of the creature that took the Prophet Muhammad (SAAS) on the Night Journey?

6. What is the name of the mosque in Jerusalem where Prophet Muhammad (SAAS) was taken to on his Night Journey from Makkah?

7. In which month was the Qur'an first revealed to the Prophet Muhammad (SAAS)?

8. On what date is Eid al-Fitr?

9. Name at least one of the places that a Muslim visits while performing Hajj.

10. What day is 10th Dhu'l Hijjah?

Background Notes

Al-Masjid al-Aqsa, Jerusalem - Literally meaning 'The Farthest Mosque', this is the third holiest mosque in Islam. Masjid al-Aqsa is not the same as the golden-coloured Dome of the Rock which is also in Jerusalem.

Al-Masjid al-Haram - Literally meaning 'The Sacred Mosque', this is the holiest mosque in Islam.

Al-Masjid an-Nabawi - Literally meaning 'The Mosque of The Prophet (SAAS)', this is the second holiest mosque in Islam.

Buraq - A heavenly riding animal described as being white, bigger than a donkey but smaller than a horse who could place his hoof as far as the eye could see (Sahih Muslim).

Dhu'l Hijjah - Literally meaning 'month of pilgrimage', this is the twelfth month of the Islamic calendar and a sacred month.

Dhu'l Qa'dah - Literally meaning 'month of rest', this is the eleventh month of the Islamic calendar and a sacred month.

Hijrah - This is the name given to the migration of the Prophet Muhammad (SAAS) and his Companions from Makkah to Madinah in the year 622 as a result of the persecution of Muslims in Makkah. This is the first year of the Islamic calendar.

Hussain bin Ali (RA) - The grandson of the Prophet Muhammad (SAAS). In 680, Yazid was made Khalifa, but some Muslims did not agree with this and believed that Hussain (RA) should be Khalifa. So these people invited Hussain (RA) to come to Kufa in Iraq, where he was told that he had support. But when he got there, the governor of Kufa had gathered an army and killed Hussain (RA) and many of his family at Karbala. This tragedy took place on 10th Muharram.

Jumada al-awwal - Literally meaning 'first freezing', this is the fifth Islamic month.

Jumada ath-thani - Literally meaning 'second freezing', this is the sixth Islamic month.

Laylat al-Isra wal Mi'raj - This is when the Prophet Muhammad (SAAS) went on a journey by night from Makkah to Jerusalem (Isra) and then up to heaven (Mi'raj) (Quran 17:1). When he returned from this incredible journey the same night, his bed was still warm!

Moon - The moon goes through phases from a new moon to a full moon and back to a new moon again. This is one lunar cycle equivalent to one lunar month (29 or 30 days). An Islamic month starts with the new moon.

Muharram - Literally meaning 'forbidden', this is the first month of the Islamic calendar and also a sacred month.

Musa (AS) - Musa (AS) led his people, the Bani Isra'il, to the Promised Land for which they had to cross the Red Sea. By Allah's permission, the sea parted for the Bani Isra'il and they were able to cross it safely, but once they had done so, the sea came together and drowned Pharaoh who was following them. This event took place on 10th Muharram. The Prophet Muhammad (SAAS) recommended that Muslims fast on this day (Sahih Muslim and Sahih Bukhari).

Nuh (AS) - Nuh (AS) was asked by Allah to build an ark and to fill it with two of every species of animal so that they could be saved from the Great Flood. After 5 months, the Ark came to rest on Mount Judi (Quran 11:44). This landing is said to have happened on 10th Muharram (Imam Ahmad).

Rabi' al-awwal - Literally meaning 'first spring', this is the third Islamic month.

Rabi' ath-thani - Literally meaning 'second spring', this is the fourth Islamic month.

Rajab - Literally meaning 'to give respect', this is the seventh Islamic month and is a sacred month.

Ramadan - Literally meaning 'intense heat', this the ninth month of the Islamic calendar in which Muslims fast from dawn to sunset.

Sacred Month - There are four 'sacred months': Muharram, Rajab, Dhu'l Qa'dah and Dhu'l Hijjah. No fighting or war is allowed during these months, except in self-defence (Quran 9:36).

Safar - Literally meaning 'empty', this is the second month of the Islamic calendar.

Salah - The Islamic prayer. Muslims are commanded to perform salah 5 times a day at fixed times. These are Fajr, Dhuhr, Asr, Maghrib and Isha.

Sha'ban - Literally meaning 'the dividing month', this the eighth month of the Islamic calendar.

Shawwal - Literally meaning 'the month of hunting', this is the tenth month of the Islamic calendar.

Zakat al-Fitr - This is a kind of charity that every Muslim must pay before the Eid prayer to purify themselves at the end of Ramadan and also help the poor (Abu Dawud and Ibn Majah).

(Note: The literal meanings of the Islamic months are named because of the climatic changes in the Arabian Peninsula at the time of the Prophet (SAAS)).